FAITH, FOOD, FREEDOM

Exploring Eating Through a Biblical Lens

Alexandra MacKillop

www.AlexandraMacKillop.com

First Printing, 2019

To my mother-in-law, who inspires me to write,

and to my sisters in Christ:

"Taste and see that the LORD is good;
blessed is the one who takes refuge in him.
Fear the LORD, you his holy people,
for those who fear him lack nothing.
The lions may grow weak and hungry,
but those who week the LORD lack no good thing."

Psalm 34:8-10

IN CHRIST, WE ARE FREE INDEED!

One of the hallmarks of the Christian faith is freedom. While we were all once enslaved to our patterns of sin, surrendering our lives to Christ allowed us to change our ways for the better. In Christ, we are no longer compelled to follow our old ways; we are able to live differently, invited into a life of freedom for God!

Today, one of the most pervasive cultural patterns is that of obsession with food and fitness. Diets and exercise plans abound, and it's easy to become overwhelmed by the countless rules about what, when, and how much to eat. However, God never intended for us to become so consumed by food; rather his desire is quite the opposite! Our purpose in life is to spread the story of his grace and glory. To do this, we each need to eat. Contrary to popular belief, the story ends there! After feeding ourselves, the next step is to get up from the table and get on with life!

Unfortunately for many women, thoughts about food continue long after dinner. In some ways, we are afraid of food, believing it to be far more powerful over our lives than it truly is. We fear that certain ingredients or meal choices will cause us to become ill or gain weight, leading us to become less valuable, less beautiful, or less able to reach our goals. But these beliefs are not from God! We read in 2 Timothy 1:7 that God does not give us a spirit of fear, but of power, love, and self-control. This means that we don't need to meticulously measure or avoid food, take pains-taking exercise efforts to find fulfillment in life, or create extra rules to make ourselves right with God. Instead, we can use food and fitness as tools for living out our callings under Christ.

In order to cultivate lives that are characterized by peace and freedom, we must ensure that we keep food in its proper place, not allowing it to consume our hearts or minds. We must reject the diet-obsessed ways of the world, transcend food preoccupations, and eat in ways that reflect trust in our bodies as well as the God who made them.

This devotional explores Christian freedom in the context of food, embracing the idea that God already gave us everything we need to cultivate holy lives -- no rules necessary! As you will learn throughout the process of this resource, eating with freedom is consistent with the calling of God on our lives to reject legalistic rules and seek the gospel above all else.

How to Use This Resource

Faith, Food, Freedom is a guided bible study that explores Christian faith as it applies to the concepts of food, dieting, and self-image. Each chapter is designed to be read on each of twenty days, and consists of a daily bible reading in the book of Galatians, a life application passage, and a series of 3-5 questions for self-reflection or group discussion.

This bible study is a helpful tool for personal growth, but is also well-suited for use in group bible studies, book studies, and mentorship meetings. It also can be used as a helpful adjunct in biblically-based counseling settings.

Why It Matters

The goal of this book is to help you cultivate awareness of the fact that dieting is not only unhelpful, but harmful as well. If in reading this book, you come to realize that your own struggles with food are affecting your life negatively, please know that you're not alone. God sees you and hears you, and wants to offer you grace, hope, and life abundant. It may take time and practice to get there, but He is faithful! [*If you are struggling to eat in a way that is honoring to God and your body, visit AlexandraMacKillop.com to learn more about how you can cultivate skills in this area of your own life and experience freedom from food rules.*]

DAY 1

◆ ◆ ◆

Galatians 1:1-10

◆ ◆ ◆

No Other Gospel

The word gospel according to Christian understanding means "good news." The message it brings is one of grace, goodness, kindness and hope; it promises that the ugly, broken parts of us are made new and beautiful by the power of God alone. Through salvation in Christ, we are liberated from the burden of shame and despair, invited to live in freedom from our sinful, worldly ways. This sense of freedom is very different from the ways of today's culture, which are filled with "should's" and "should not's," many of which are inconsistent with what God asks of us.

Whenever we feed into the beliefs of the world about what makes us lovable, valuable, or special, we are living out the lie that something else other than Christ holds the power of salvation. In effect, we are professing a different gospel from the gospel of Christ. Some of these false gospels include those of our internal thought lives, including perfectionism, people-pleasing, and an obsession with physical appearance or modern trends. Believing that we need something more than holistic trust in Christ to find our worth goes against the core belief of the "good news gospel" that defines our faith.

Reflections

1. In verse 4, we read that Jesus's sacrifice on the cross rescued us from the evils of this age. What are some of the evils of this age that you've encountered, from which you've experienced the rescuing power of God?

2. Many of the ways of the world call us away from gospel truth. What are some ways that our cultural dieting obsessions draw us away from Christ?

3. How do diets present themselves as false gospels? What are some examples of lies that you've been tempted to believe about life or about your worth? (These can be related to food, fitness, or any other area of life.)

4. How can a dieting obsession feed into the temptation to "try to win the approval of human beings" rather than God, as described in verse 10?

5. In verse 10, Paul calls himself a "servant of Christ." What are some ways that your temptations with food (or otherwise) detract from your ability to fulfill your calling toward servanthood under Christ?

DAY 2

◆ ◆ ◆

Galatians 1:11-14

◆ ◆ ◆

Turning Away

W hen we commit to faith in Christ, we become new creations. Our hearts are changed, our minds are changed, and our lives are changed. The things that once captivated us do so no longer, and our behaviors, habits and interests are likewise redeemed. Our belief in Christ is transformative and all-encompassing, redefining us completely.

In this passage, Paul describes his "previous way of life" and the habits that used to define him. He persecuted Christians, living out the lies and falsehoods of the world for an agenda that had captivated his heart. While most of us today don't have a history like that of Paul, we too were once defined by sin. Although we might be tempted to feel shame or disgust with the details of our old lives, the stories of our pasts provide a powerful testimony to the transformational ability of the gospel. (This is especially true when we begin living out a new life of freedom.) The work that God has done in our lives is far less *about us* than it is *about Him*. The weakness of who we once were points to the strength of who God is. So, in reflecting on the transformations that God has already done, we are given hope for what He promises to do in us and through us in the future.

Reflections

1. In verse 11, Paul reminds us that the gospel is not of human origin. What are some of the ways through which you are reminded of the supernatural power of the gospel?

2. In the bible, we read that Paul was converted to Christian faith through a divine vision given to him by God. While the same is true of others today, we each are called to Christ in unique ways. Reflect on the process of your own salvation – how did you become convinced of the truth of Christ?

3. In his reflections on his previous way of life, Paul gives specifics of his worldly behavior. How does your relationship with food reflect the patterns of your old sinful ways?

4. Which qualities of dieting captivate you? How do thoughts related to food and fitness detract from your ability to fulfill God's calling on your life?

DAY 3

◆ ◆ ◆

Galatians 1:15-24

◆ ◆ ◆

A New Life

After experiencing his revelation, Paul immediately began acting on his new faith in two specific ways: first, he leaned into the guidance of God; second, he began sharing about his new passion.

Our Christian faith touches on every aspect of our lives. However, it can sometimes be difficult to sift through the cultural chatter and identify God's voice with regards to our present concerns. This is especially true in the area of food and health, as society's views on the matter are announced loudly from every avenue. God's voice, though perhaps quieter, is revealed clearly in his word. Like Paul, whenever we trust God with a new area of our lives, it's essential that we lean into His truth and tune out distractions. As these changes manifest in our hearts, minds, and actions, the transformation in us becomes evident to those around us. Truly, a person cannot change as dramatically on his or her own accord as when he or she comes to faith in Christ. This becomes evident to others, whether they share the same beliefs or not, and can create the opportunity to share God's truth.

◆ ◆ ◆

Reflections

1. In verse 15, Paul refers to himself as set apart by grace. When we reject diet culture and enjoy food freely, we are setting ourselves apart from the larger culture. Why is it important for us, as Christians, to be set apart in every aspect of our lives?

2. When Paul was given a new mission by God, he didn't first consult other people; he consulted God. What are some areas of your life in which you elevate the opinion of others over that of God? Do you do this with your beliefs about food?

3. If a person having a long history of dieting were to reject these ways and start exercising freedom in his or her eating, how would this behavior appear to outsiders? Would this testimony of freedom point others toward or away from Christ?

DAY 4

◆ ◆ ◆

Galatians 2:1-5

◆ ◆ ◆

Purity in Truth

After Paul had been working in his ministry for a number of years, he experienced a time of faltering in his beliefs. While he didn't altogether renounce his faith, he was experiencing a time of questioning and doubt. Like so many of the rest of us, he needed some encouragement that what he was professing was good, right, and true. In seeking reinforcement from others, Paul's faith, drive and purpose were strengthened. At the same time as Paul and Titus were able to be encouraged and supported by other Christian leaders, they were able to address the common problem of false beliefs, legalistic practices, and condemning attitudes. These cultural beliefs were not only causing community members to question themselves, but they were even causing experienced leaders like Paul to struggle, too.

Experiencing times of doubt and questioning does not mean we are bad Christians, and it doesn't mean we are condemned. God understands our struggles; they are common among church members throughout history. When you find yourself struggling to trust God with his call on your life to live in freedom, lean into your faith seek accountability, and most importantly, pray.

Reflections

1. Have there ever been times you questioned your faith? What was the result? Were your beliefs strengthened or weakened after this season?

2. Consider the times you've struggled in your beliefs about food. Were your beliefs about the role of food in your life strengthened or weakened in this time? If these experiences frustrated you, what does this teach you about the fleeting nature of food and fitness claims as compared to the eternal truths of God?

3. What are some of the ways that diet culture distorts the truth about who God says we are? (This could be related to eating habits, body image, or our value and worth as humans.)

4. What is the risk of embracing a pattern of dieting rather than the role for food that God intended? (See verse 4b)

DAY 5

◆ ◆ ◆

Galatians 2:6-10

◆ ◆ ◆

Equality in Christ

Each of us individually made the choice to become Christians, and for each of us, this decision took place at a different time. Likewise, at any given point in time, we each have a different level of understanding about faith, theology, and the nature of God. Growing in this understanding is referred to as the process of sanctification, which can also be understood to mean *maturing in our faith*.

However, it's important to recognize that no matter our level of maturity in faith, God does not show favoritism. He does not value mature Christians any more than he values new Christians – we have all been His children since the beginning of time.

Just as we may sometimes compare ourselves to others in terms of our religious maturity, we may also be tempted to compare ourselves to each other in terms of our relationship with food. We may covet the bodies of others based off their respective shape or size, or we may envy the way that our neighbors make food choices. In these times of doubt or comparison, remind yourself that you are uniquely created to be beautiful – just like everyone else.

We each are at a different place in our understanding of this truth and God is continually working within each of us – both those of us who struggle to keep food in its proper place, as well as in those of us who have been skilled in this area for years.

Reflections

1. Have you ever been tempted to compare yourselves to others in the realm(s) of faith or food matters? If so, what were some of the specific areas you noticed? How can you use awareness of this tendency toward comparison to compel you to protect yourself against these temptations?

2. What does it look like to have a relationship with food that is not honoring to God? What does it look like to have a relationship with food that is honoring to God? What steps can you take today to help restore your eating patterns to those that are reflective of God's glory?

3. In today's passage, Paul explained how the issue of circumcision created a distraction in his ability to carry out his purpose in life. How do food struggles and comparisons detract from your ability to fulfill God's calling on your life?

DAY 6

◆ ◆ ◆

Galatians 2:11-14

◆ ◆ ◆

Opposing the World

When we choose to live for Christ, we are called to be bold and courageous in our faith. Sometimes this simply requires that we keep up with the type of lifestyle that God calls us towards, and other times it means we need to stand up and fight against cultural patterns of sin. In this passage, we read that Paul openly opposed Cephas because his behavior of ostracizing gentiles was contrary to the inclusive nature of the gospel.

Many of our culture's diet obsessions come from a place of idolatry and legalism, meaning they suggest that we need something more than trust in Christ to be valuable and worthy. This often stems from the idea that thin bodies are more beautiful, and that a person's diet (or body weight) represents their internal characteristics, such as: laziness vs. responsibility, gluttony vs. self-control, or diligence vs. self-neglect. In viewing certain dietary practices or body shapes as superior, we create a sense of exclusion, sometimes without even realizing it. Eating according to certain rules or following a particular diet plan does not make a person more worthy, loveable, or "holy." Be careful not to assign spiritual weight to the practice of eating that God doesn't assign.

Reflections

1. Have you noticed any patterns in your social circles in which certain body shapes or dietary rules are viewed as superior? Compare this to what the gospel says about eating and body diversity.

2. When we separate ourselves from others by viewing our behavior as superior, what is the spiritual risk of this? How does this behavior point others toward the gospel, or pull them away from it?

3. Our behaviors are influential – we can inspire other people to act like we do just by hanging around them. How have your diet habits (or the language you use about food) pointed others towards the all-encompassing love of God? Do they point others away?

DAY 7

◆ ◆ ◆

Galatians 2:15-18

◆ ◆ ◆

By Faith Alone

When we become Christians, God calls us to live differently. We are invited into his love, which empowers us to turn away from the sinful practices that once defined us and instead embrace a new identity in Christ. Knowing that we are to be defined by holiness, it's easy to fall into the belief that unless we are successful at behaving as Christ calls us to behave, we are not truly Christians. In other words, we sometimes believe that we are saved because we act like we have been saved. However, the message of truth and love that we encounter in the gospel is that we are valuable not because of what we do but because of who we are: beloved daughters of the King.

Believing that our actions hold the power of salvation can sometimes extend beyond even the types of actions commonly seen as "spiritual" – like praying, serving, or tithing. Sometimes we view ourselves as more worthy because we are successful at avoiding sweets, exercising regularly, or eating salads. We see these behaviors as good, and likewise view ourselves as good for engaging in them. But the truth of the gospel is that we are made special, loveable, and worthy not because of anything we do, but because of what God does through his grace and kindness.

Reflections

1. What does it mean to you that God loves you because of who you are rather than what you do? What are some of the ways in which you've been tempted to believe that your actions or behaviors ("works") are what save you?

2. Sometimes Christ calls us to engage with other people who are not Christians. Other times, we can protect ourselves spiritually by avoiding certain people or situations. How have the people in your life encouraged you towards Christ? How have they tempted you toward sin?

3. What are some of the ways that engaging in diet behavior has fostered guilt and shame in your life? Given what we know about faith being the most important thing for our salvation, is this guilt and shame validated? Does God shame you the same way you shame yourself?

DAY 8

◆ ◆ ◆

Galatians 2:19-21

◆ ◆ ◆

By Faith Alone

B efore Jesus came to earth, life under God looked very different. In the Old Testament, the people of Israel were responsible for following a vast number of extremely strict laws which were designed to set them apart from the rest of the world and mark them as God's own. However, the intensity of these many laws made it very difficult for anyone to follow them completely. In fact, nobody could! The purpose of these laws wasn't merely to be followed, but more so to demonstrate that without the help of God, humans are not capable of achieving perfection in this life. We all desperately need Jesus.

Extreme diet rules can cause us to feel the same sense of hopelessness and frustration as the laws of the Old Testament – unless we remember that rules can't make us healthier, happier, or holier. When we accept Christ as the savior for our sins, we are set free from the laws of the Old Testament and granted freedom to live by faith. Living by faith means trusting that it is Christ alone that saves us and satisfies us. If dietary rules, or any other type for that matter, had the power to save or satisfy – "if righteousness could be gained through the law" (verse 21) – then we would have no need for Christ.

Reflections

1. The purpose of the Old Testament Law was to teach us that we are powerless to live perfectly without the help of Christ. When you create extra rules around your own life, do they help you feel empowered or ashamed?

2. What does it mean to die to the law? (Verse 19)

3. When we live by faith in our bodies, as we read about in verse 20, this means that we can trust God to equip us to live for him. What does it mean to you to trust God with your body?

4. In verse 21 we are called to remember the grace of God, which is our true source of righteousness. In what ways do you need to remind yourself of the grace of God? How might grace help set you free in terms of your relationship with food and your body?

DAY 9

◆ ◆ ◆

Galatians 3:1-6

◆ ◆ ◆

Faith > Works

Even after we become Christians, we are still faced with the temptation to sin. The people of Galatia faced this same temptation – specifically through legalism. Legalism refers to the practice of regarding certain practices as necessary for salvation even though Jesus never said they were necessary in the Christian life. (We know that we are saved by faith alone.) In this passage, Paul is lecturing the Galatians because even though they were saved by their faith, they started to deviate from the core of the gospel by saying that further actions were needed -- in addition to faith -- in order for a person to be saved.

In today's day and age, we tend to fall into the same sorts of patterns as the Galatians – albeit inadvertently. This is especially true with food. Even though most people would agree that following a certain diet can't save us in the way that Jesus does, we still feel guilty and ashamed when we deviate from our self-imposed food rules. These include rules about the type of foods we eat, the quantities we serve ourselves, and when. Limits like "only eating dessert on weekends," "no food after 7 pm" and "low carb" are all examples of food rules, but none of them are able to grant us the happiness or satisfaction we truly crave.

Reflections

1. Consider the advertisements about diets and weight loss that you've seen throughout your life. What do you think is the motivation behind them? Are these motivations to push you towards Godliness or towards worldliness? (In other words, is the purpose of the advertisement to help you become more like Christ, or to turn a profit?)

2. What are some of the ways that you seek to "earn" your own salvation through works rather than by surrendering in faith? These examples could pertain to food or to any other area of life.

3. Consider the way you approach food. Do your thoughts and behaviors surrounding eating empower you to further the kingdom of God or do they create barriers and distractions?

4. In verse 6, we read that Abraham "believed God, and it was credited to him as righteousness." What does God say about food? When we believe this, how does it transform our lives?

DAY 10

◆ ◆ ◆

Galatians 3:7-14

◆ ◆ ◆

Inheriting Holiness

In this passage, we read that on account of our faith we can be considered "children of Abraham." This is because Abraham was the first person to be saved through hope in Christ. Even though Abraham has long since passed from the earth, he set a legacy for us by trusting in God. In this way, he can be considered a model figure in our faith. Abraham was considered a holy and righteous man, so we should seek to emulate his characteristics in our own lives.

The faith of Abraham is the same faith of Christians today. Likewise, the humanity of Abraham is the same humanity we face today – we have all the same needs, the same fears, the same trials, and the same temptations. Yet despite his *human-ness* he remained strong in his faith, relying on hope in God rather than trying to take control of his own life by enacting his own plans. We should all strive to do likewise.

Perhaps you find yourself struggling to embrace the body that God created uniquely for you, along with all its cravings, its wrinkles, or its soft spots. But our hope in life is not found in the flesh but in the promises of Christ. Because God created our bodies in the image of Christ, we can trust them! One of the promises of our faith is that regardless of our appearances, we are dearly loved – made holy and righteous by Christ alone.

Reflections

1. In the beginning, God created Adam and Eve. In the same way, he created Abraham, and likewise he created each of us. He has not changed his ways from the original two humans that he placed in the Garden of Eden. How does knowing that God created us purposefully and with wisdom influence the way you view your own body?

2. In verse 13, we read that Christ redeemed us from the curse of the law by dying on the cross. However, every time we create unnecessary, new laws (especially those about diet rules) we are living out a life of sin, metaphorically nailing Christ to the cross all over again. How does this illustration motivate you to reject legalistic rules and live by faith?

3. In verse 14, we read that through faith in Christ, we receive the promise of the Spirit. What is this promise that we receive?

DAY 11

◆ ◆ ◆

Galatians 3:15-22

◆ ◆ ◆

Our Promise

This passage describes the bold ways in which Abraham was obedient and faithful toward God, even in circumstances that were difficult for him – such as being asked to sacrifice his own son. Even though following God would have been painful for Abraham, he was still willing to do what he was called to do. True faith means trusting God even when you disagree with him.

Perhaps you are currently struggling to honor the body that God gave you, or perhaps honor the way of eating that God calls us toward (responding appropriately to hunger and fullness cues, for example). Choosing to eat in a balanced way when we are dissatisfied with our bodies may feel challenging, but it is the right thing to do – and we are empowered to do so through faith in Christ.

In verse 22, we read that through faith in Jesus Christ, we are free from the control of sin. Through faith, we are empowered to turn away from the things that once enslaved us, locked us up, and created distance between us and God. Through faith, we are able to experience the promises of God. Through faith, we are able to see where true joy and fulfillment come from.

Reflections

1. Like Abraham, sometimes God asks us to do things that feel challenging, scary, or painful. What are some of the calls of God on your life today that are difficult for you to respond faithfully towards?

2. In this passage, we read that the law points out the sin in our lives. What this means is that the Old Testament rules were impossible to follow perfectly – that was obvious to everybody! However, in the death and resurrection of Christ, the Israelites were absolved of their shortcomings. Do you find that you are struggling to follow through with God's call on your life today? Share them with God in prayer. Ask him to equip you to live rightly.

3. In Christ, we are free to experience true joy. Have you been tempted to look to other things in life for joy or purpose, such as food? What would it look like to live differently?

DAY 12

◆ ◆ ◆

Galatians 3:23-29

◆ ◆ ◆

Children of God

"Guardianship of the law" refers to the idea that the laws of the old testament were playing a role – they were teaching us something. They served a purpose for that time, but now that their purpose has been fulfilled, we are set free. We can think about dieting the same way. For a time, dieting may have seemed to fulfill a need in your life. Maybe it made you feel in control, helped you lose weight, or gave you direction when you didn't know where else to turn. But dieting wasn't the end-all-be-all. It didn't solve all your problems, and it didn't even solve many of the problems it claimed it could solve. After a period of dieting, we often feel out of control again – we regain the weight, we lose direction, we become frustrated. Dieting may have helped you for a season, but that season is likely over. Now, there is a new purpose for each of us that is far bigger than any of the superficial identities we may have claimed in the past. Our identity in Christ is far bigger than things like thinness, fitness, or physical beauty – it is eternal.

Reflections

1. If you're a former dieter, creating rules around food likely helped you in the beginning. What were some of the positive benefits you found that dieting gave you in your life?

2. As is the case with diets, eventually the rules become impossible to follow. When your diet started failing you, how did this make you feel? About yourself? About God?

3. In Christ, it doesn't matter if we "eat clean" or "Paleo" or "Vegan" or "Atkins" – or any of the other labels we allow food to give us. What does it mean for you to be set free from these empty labels?

4. What's the difference between honoring God in your approach to food, and idolizing food?

5. Sometimes, we don't realize an idol is what it is -- we can't see in the moment that it's taking over our lives. But if we consider how we spend our time and money, we can see things more clearly. What in your life do you spend the most time and money on? How much time and money do you spend on diet foods, exercise plans, gym memberships, and body-sculpting shape wear?

DAY 13

◆ ◆ ◆

Galatians 4:1-7

◆ ◆ ◆

We Are Heirs

"When you know better, you do better."
Just like immaturity sometimes leads children to make wrong choices, we sometimes sin as adults because we lack the foresight needed to understand the long-term, eternal consequences of our actions. When we sin, it is sometimes out of a sense of spiritual immaturity. If we fully understood how the story ends, we wouldn't be drawn to the fleeting temptations of now. It can be easy to condemn ourselves for our past mistakes – especially when those mistakes lead to ongoing consequences. Sometimes our sins continue to affect us, even long after we've turned away from them. However, the beautiful truth of the gospel is that even though we may be facing the consequences of sin in our lives, our faith in God makes it such that no matter how bad our past behavior was, God's present love for us is unchanged.

Reflections

1. What are some lies about yourself (or life in general) that you used to believe prior to experiencing saving faith in Christ?

2. Specifically, what are some of the lies you believed about the merits of dieting? How have those since been invalidated? If you still find yourself drawn towards dieting, where might you look to see what God says about the matter?

3. Do you find yourself wrestling with shame and regret with regards to your choices involving food and exercise? What does God say about our past mistakes?

4. Verse 7 discusses how as children of God, we are able to inherit His kingdom and everything in it – we don't have to do anything to "earn" God's favor! How does this transform the way you see yourself?

5. Consider the way you presently approach food, your body, and exercise. If you continue on exactly as you are, by the time you reach the end of your life, will you have any regrets?

DAY 14

◆ ◆ ◆

Galatians 4:8-16

◆ ◆ ◆

Not into Temptation

Prior to becoming Christians, we were led astray by the deceit of sin. The world fed us lies that in order to be valuable, find purpose, or cultivate happiness, we needed to accumulate material gains. These gains manifest as money, "stuff," hobbies, and even the gains of cultural beauty. In today's day and age, this often involves a fit and trim physique, following a strict diet plan, trendy clothes and carefully applied makeup.

In the excitement of new or revived faith, it feels easy to follow God. Our hearts tend more towards holiness and spiritual gain rather than the temptations of the world around us. But, seasons come and go. For many of us, we eventually find ourselves returning to the things that once so captivated our attention.

In moments of frustration, boredom and weakness, we fall prey to the idea that in order to be more worthy or valuable, we need to change our bodies. These lies can creep in slowly, planting seeds that sprout days, weeks, or months later, leading us to become preoccupied with the things of the flesh rather than the things of God.

Reflections

1. When you first became a Christian, how did your thought patterns change? What did you spend most of your time thinking about? What were your main priorities?

2. As time went on, did you notice that the things that once enslaved you started to slowly become interesting again? How did you (or do you) respond to those temptations?

3. What are some of the influences in your life that affect your view of food, dieting and exercise?

4. What are some safeguards that you can put into place to prevent against temptation in these areas – food, or otherwise?

DAY 15

◆ ◆ ◆

Galatians 4:17-31

◆ ◆ ◆

Who You Follow

In verse 17, Paul refers to false teachers who were supposing to have religious authority but were not preaching truth. These individuals were often all about following rules, and they'd sell the idea that strict adherence to these rules would bring happiness. However, these teachers were not concerned with holiness, but rather with their own popularity and building their own kingdoms of fame. Though appealing, these rules had nothing to do with the gospel. Paul compared followers of these false teachers and the opposite, followers of Christ, to two women: Hagar and Sarah. Individuals who fall prey to deception and lies (such as Hagar) are destined to slavery. On the contrary, those who are committed to scripture and spiritual health (like Sarah) are invited into a lifetime of freedom.

Diet companies are built upon their ability to sell products, gain a following, and make money. The more the businesses can sell their ideas, the more money they will make. Dieting and food obsessions aren't about holiness, they're about creating slaves that will be lifetime buyers of thinness, food plans, and exercise obsessions. But those who are able to see beyond the lies of diet culture are set free to live for things that are far more important.

Reflections

1. When you consider your own spiritual life, do you find that you are drawn to following rules? Why or why not?

2. In the Bible, we read that our salvation is not dependent on what we do or don't do, or on how well we follow rules; it's simply about complete surrender of our own strength and abilities to the redemptive power of Christ. How does this challenge your own beliefs or habits?

3. Do you find that you look to food rules for comfort? What benefits do you see in your own life from following food rules? In what ways do you find it harms you?

4. Would you consider *following food rules* to be a practice that enslaves you, or a practice that sets you free?

DAY 16

◆ ◆ ◆

Galatians 5:1-12

◆ ◆ ◆

Freedom in Christ

In Matthew 6:24, we read that it's impossible to serve two masters (both God and money.) The same holds true for following *both* Christ *and* the ways of the world – the two perspectives mutually invalidate each other. When considering the pressures of today's culture, everything is "me-centered." All of our worldly callings are to do more, look better, feel happier, and promote ourselves. Things like selflessness, compassion, submission and servitude are unimportant. On the other hand, the calling of Christ is to forget outward appearances and turn away from anything that distracts us from the most important thing: love.

In this passage, Paul explains that in Christ, the things of the world have no value, no matter how appealing they may seem. Every step toward cultural values alienates us from Christ, pulling us away from the grace that sets us free. Our faith is like yeast that we knead through the dough of our lives; The same is true of worldly views and practices – allowing a little bit in allows it to take over our whole selves.

◆ ◆ ◆

Reflections

1. Think about the culture you currently live in. Which character qualities, attitudes, and behaviors are considered valuable? Which are considered undesirable?

2. Now consider your faith – which character qualities, attitudes, and behaviors does God value? Which ones does he condemn?

3. In verse 7, Paul writes, "You were running a good race. Who cut in on you to keep you from obeying the truth?" What are some of the influences that draw you away from God and tempt you to live in the ways of the world?

4. Which specific influences do you encounter that tempt you to micromanage your food and exercise habits, start a new diet, and turn back to the things that once enslaved you?

DAY 17

◆ ◆ ◆

Galatians 5:13-26

◆ ◆ ◆

Life by the Spirit

All of us are sinful – each and every one of us. We desire popularity, beauty, perfection, superiority and total control. But these things are not only unattainable, they are never things we are called to pursue in Christ. Dieting for the purpose of beauty stems from an unhealthy comparison game – we feel ashamed of ourselves because we see a more beautiful or thinner woman on the street. Instead of finding satisfaction with the purpose and callings that God has given uniquely to us in life, we desire to be the thinner or more beautiful woman, and to live her life instead of ours. But indulging this dog-eat-dog, jealousy-driven, vanity competition will destroy us (verse 15).

Instead of falling prey to the dieting game, we are invited to walk by the spirit, avoiding things that lay a breeding ground for sin and instead seek to manifest the fruits of the spirit in our lives: love, joy, peace, patience, kindness, goodness, faithfulness, gentleness and self-control. Belonging to Christ means crucifying our desires to strive for beauty, fitness and thinness, and instead work toward spiritual rather than physical gain.

Reflections

1. Criticizing our appearance (or that of others) never stems from love; it comes from envy, judgement, and condemnation. Do you find yourself focusing on your own flaws and comparing them to the gifts you seen in other people? Confess this practice to God.

2. Rather than focusing on the qualities you dislike about yourself, focus on the how you can strive towards godliness. What would it look like to put love, joy, peace, patience, kindness, gentleness, faithfulness and self-control into practice? Make a list of these qualities and how you can cultivate them in your own attitudes and behaviors.

3. When we are living for God, our strength to do so is driven by the Holy Spirit. What are some examples of times when you've noticed the Holy Spirit nudging you? How did you know it was the Holy Spirit?

DAY 18

◆ ◆ ◆

Galatians 6:1-10

◆ ◆ ◆

Good to All

Many of us know that helping others is a good thing to do – but this also means that receiving help when we need it is a good thing, too! It's okay to admit that we need help sometimes, and it's okay to ask for it from those we trust. Being able to give and receive help necessitates that we aren't comparing ourselves to others. If we or others are afraid of being judged for our shortcomings, we will never be able to make progress towards health and healing. Even if we fall short of expectations, we are covered by the grace of God to start afresh and try again.

However, when we set out to cultivate new habits and attitudes in our lives, we will not be able to make progress if we keep doing what we've always done. In other words, we reap what we sow. In this passage, Paul explains that we can't live in the ways of the world, tell ourselves that we are actually living for Christ, and then assume that everything will be fine. In order to truly live for God and experience a fulfilling life, we need to do the dirty work of being honest with ourselves and others about our motives. Only then can we cultivate true healing and reap the joy of holiness.

Reflections

1. Are there areas of your life in which you are struggling to live as you know God would prefer? Who can you seek help from for accountability, mentorship, or Biblically grounded advice?

2. Have you ever been wary to share your heart with someone for fear of being judged? Have you ever made others feel this way? What does it look like to offer a sincere and listening ear for those who need guidance?

3. In life, we reap what we sow. Consider the areas of your life that you're dissatisfied with. What actions did you take in the past that brought you to this point? What can you do today to start planting seeds for a better tomorrow?

DAY 19

◆ ◆ ◆

Galatians 6:11-18

◆ ◆ ◆

The New Creation

In this passage, Paul was referring to the fact that some Jewish leaders were putting too much emphasis on circumcision, believing that it was the only proof of true holiness. However, at the same time, they were completely ignoring other Jewish laws which were equally important in the Old Testament.

Many of us do the same thing today. While we may not be considering things like circumcision, we scoff at behaviors like drunkenness or sexual deviance but ignore equally harmful things like hatred, gossip or envy.

This is especially true with regards to sinful attitudes toward food – many people hail dieting as a good thing because it seems to be the polar opposite of gluttony. However, just as dangerous as gluttony is an obsession with thinness, dietary control, weight loss, clean eating, or counting calories. These habits can easily become idolatrous, but they aren't typically talked about that way.

Just like binge eating brownies in an attempt to fill a need for Christ in our lives is sinful (because such a practice is gluttonous), taking painstaking measures to avoid desserts or snacks for the sake of weight loss is also sinful; a thinner body will not fulfill us, either.

Reflections

1. Do you find that you focus on avoiding certain sins in your life, but completely ignore others? What would it look like to turn away from the sins you often overlook?

2. In your experiences with dieting and weight-loss, have you ever considered that pursuing these things might be sinful? If not, why do you think that is?

3. What do you believe God thinks about enjoying desserts, eating snacks, or partaking in a relaxing activity like a bubble bath or a nap? How are these self-care activities typically viewed in our culture?

4. It's easy to get caught up in the external appearance of our behaviors – dieting seems righteous; pizza seems sinfully delicious. How are these ideas true? How are they false? What are the spiritual implications of them?

DAY 20

◆ ◆ ◆

Eat with Freedom

Think about how you currently make decisions about food. What influences your choices? Do you consider what you've already eaten that day? Do you pay attention to information you've heard on television, seen on billboards, or read on social media? Do you think about your body's shape and size, shame yourself, or try to use food as a means for manipulating your appearance?

These are common habits of people in today's society, likely because those patterns define what we've been taught all our lives. But, frustratingly, they don't make our lives better. These food rules make eating a stressful experience. When God created humans, he never intended for eating to be such a difficult task. It was supposed to sustain our lives, not drain them!

Proverbs 3:19-20 reads: "By wisdom the Lord laid the earth's foundations, by understanding he set the heavens in place; by his knowledge the watery depths were divided, and the clouds let drop the dew." The same is true with our bodies.

God knew what he was doing when he created humans. Each

step was intentional, each organ has its own special role, and all of our systems work together in a beautiful, graceful way – no interventions needed! Physiologically, we function as we were designed to function, all on our own, or at least inasmuch as God permits! Likewise, our bodies are all unique shapes and sizes, and when we eat in a way that honors them, we are able to settle in to happy, healthy, holy lives. When we're distracted by food, we can't live fully for God; but when we keep food in its proper place, we're set free to pursue the things in life that are far more important than food!

Reflections

1. Do you find that the way you make decisions about food or your body is draining your life? What would it mean for you to begin approaching food and exercise differently?

2. Consider what you learned about Christian freedom in this study of Galatians. How can you apply your God-given freedom to your patterns of eating?

3. Have you ever been told that you could look exactly the way you wanted if you only ate a certain way, exercised a certain amount, or followed a certain plan? How does this idea compare to the truth that God created you uniquely?

4. Is the idea of eating with freedom new to you? Does it appeal to you, or not? What is your next step?

ABOUT THE AUTHOR

Alexandra MacKillop is a food scientist, and primary health-care provider at a holistic clinic near Chicago, IL. She is passionate about helping women cultivate lifestyle behaviors that honor both God and their bodies through a non-diet approach to nutrition and wellness. In addition to clinical practice, she writes about her experiences with faith, food, and medicine on her blog, AlexandraMacKillop.com. Through her writing, she ultimately seeks to encourage others to love God and live fully for Him.

◆ ◆ ◆

Bible passages in this devotional are from the
New International Version (NIV).